MEMORIES OF A CHILDHOOD IN MICHIGAN

NASSER ABUHAMDA

authorHOUSE

AuthorHouse™
1663 Liberty Drive
Bloomington, IN 47403
www.authorhouse.com
Phone: 833-262-8899

Published by AuthorHouse 08/25/2021

ISBN: 978-1-6655-3629-5 (sc)
ISBN: 978-1-6655-3628-8 (e)

Print information available on the last page.

We all remember those fond memories that we had as kids growing up, whether it was in a big city or a small town, there would be those special moments in time that we tend to cherish and hold on to, we do so because they mean so much to us.

Upon visiting my old town years later, I was surprised to see just how little my town had changed, and that is what brought back so much of those fond moments.

And it is this reason which brought me to write this book, to share with you some of the crazy and memorable moments that I had growing up in Michigan.

CHAPTER 1

MY EARLY YEARS

Growing up in Dearborn Michigan in the early 70s was a great time for me, I was about six years old when I started my little adventures and having two sisters plus great friends helped make that possible. Dearborn a blue-collar suburban area was where everyone pretty much knew who their neighbors were, and having good neighbors was very important, especially for a kid my age.

I didn't know it then until much later in life, just how famous and historic my town actually was, after all that's where Henry Ford started his manufacturing plant for the model T and is still in operation today. And most of the people in town pretty much relied on that factory for work. There was also the Henry Ford Museum and the Ford village which is a great tourist destination today.

My uncle who also worked at the factory would sometimes get a lift from his friend that worked for the Coca-Cola Company, and would stop by with his company truck to give us some free soda in which was great to have, especially on a hot summer day.

Summertime was a very special time for me, all the kids would be out as usual, some riding their bikes others on their rollerblades, as for me I couldn't do either one. But I managed to find some areas of interest, and of course some of my interests would be a little out of the ordinary.

At a very early age I discovered that sometimes you would learn a lot on your own, and I was one that would always venture out looking for some adventures. Having a pretty big yard, I would love roaming around looking for all types of bugs and insects, such as grasshoppers, Beatles, crickets and anything else that would come my way.

On some occasions I would carry a glass jar for when I would catch these little critters, then I would put them inside the jar and stuff some grass and twigs along with them, I would do this to see how they would react with each other. Sometimes I would take Beatles and put them into puddles of water to watch how they would swim across, to my surprise I had learned that certain insects was able to walk on the surface of water, later I got interested in other insects to watch how they would react in certain environments.

One of my favorites was the praying mantis which I was very fond of, I was very interested of the details on him with its long arms in which it used to grab its prey, and the giant wings when flying around. I would love to watch how he would catch and eat up the other insects, for me It was very fascinating to see how it would do this, and I would later learn a great deal about how the strong would overcome the weak.

My backyard also had many fruit trees, such as apple and pear trees and even some peach and cherry tree's. I say this because when the fruits were ripe for picking my mother would ask us to climb up and fill them with the fruits. However, the bags weren't only for ourselves but for some of the neighbors that would come by for the fruits.

Now it never bothered me to do this because I would love to see the expressions on their faces when they got them, they would smile and thank you for the fruits – but I believe they were smiling because it was for free.

We also had a garage behind the house that my mother barely used, the garage was at the very back of the yard where the alleyway would be. Many times, me and my friends would climb up the garage and hang out on top. One day we decided to make a small clubhouse on top of it, we used a ladder to bring up some materials and managed to put together a small but comfortable hang out spot, now we had this clubhouse for several days, that is until One of my friends had fallen off, luckily for him it wasn't serious.

After the incident my mother stopped us because she thought it was too dangerous for us to be up so high. Much later we decided to make a clubhouse on the inside of the garage, however that would become a whole different experience. – –

Now behind our house we had an alleyway that went behind all the other houses on the block, for me it looked like it never ended. We would have great memories in this alleyway and quite a few adventures as well. However, there was also a very large field beyond the alleyway which looked like it went on forever, there were no homes on this field – reason for that is, it was used as a buffer zone to separate the residential areas and a quarry factory. Now this field was supposed to be off limits to everyone especially kids, of course being curious and inquisitive kids that we were, we would venture inside this field many times, upon doing so we would get into situations and have experiences that would change my outlook in life.

CHAPTER 2

MY SCHOOL YEARS

School was always a fun time for me, whether it was activities in class or outside at the playground, there was always something to do. Now waking up for school was a whole different matter, I would try and give my mother all sorts of excuses as not to go. However once there and seeing all your friends would change all that. Once together with your friends felt like, you were in a special place, and only you and your friends understood how it felt to be together.

The schoolyard was a great place to be, there was a small courtyard where the kids would line up in the mornings before going to class, however then there was the larger yard behind the school where we would have our recess time after lunch. I loved this yard because besides the playground there was a large hill where me and my friends would run up to – now right across the hill there was a railroad yard that was used by the Ford factory –

The trains would transport coal deposits and other minerals to the factory, my friends and I would love watching them. One day while on the hill we spotted a praying mantis, now I was very fascinated by insects especially that of the praying mantis, so on this day we decided to grab the mantis and show it off to the rest of the class, especially the girls.

Now as you can imagine the girls not too fond of this, ran away yelling their heads off.

One day during recess there was a situation that occurred to our assistant teacher Ms. Nichols. Now to tell you the truth she reminded me of Cap'n Crunch – which is a cereal for kids. As we were playing around, I suddenly heard some kids screaming. As I turned to see what was going on, I noticed that Ms. Nichols was flat on the floor and couldn't get back up.

We walked over to see what had happened, as we got closer, I could see Ms. Nichols on the floor and struggling to get up. She had tripped and broken her ankle. There all around her were a bunch of kids crying, all of them girls including my teacher.

Moments later the ambulance arrived, as you can imagine the girls along with our teacher stood there crying and all shaken up. Days later my teacher stated that we were going to go over to see Ms. Nichols in the hospital, upon arriving, – there laying in her bed was Ms. Nichols, with a great big cast on her leg.

Ms. Nichols asked us to sign her cast which we all did – however, my friend who happened to have a beetle on him allowed the beetle to enter the cast through where her foot was.

Where did he get the beetle I never found out – Let's just say that it was a memorable moment.

Now my school was not just for kids of my age in which I started at six years old, the classes started from kindergarten up to sixth graders and for me that's what made it even more interesting. Being in a school with such an age difference you tend to pick up good and bad habits from the older kids, and sometimes these habits would reflect on you later in life, and it also would teach me some lessons as to taking care of yourself when the odds were against you. –

As in one case my class was having lunch in the cafeteria, now I don't know what happened but the older kids were also there. Now they had separated the older kids from the younger ones, but with my mind wandering around and not paying attention, I had gone over to stand online for lunch not knowing it was reserved for the older grades. After grabbing my tray, I somehow went over to the six graders table, all nervous and confused I didn't have a clue of where I was and simply stood in the middle of the cafeteria frozen. –

Then an older girl who I guess was a monitor approached me and asked if I would like to sit down with the older kids, not knowing what I was doing I went straight over to them. As she escorted me over to the table, that is when I saw all these strange faces staring at me. To tell you the truth I felt a bit frightened to see so many strange faces all staring at me. A few minutes later an older kid came up to me and asked what was I doing here. –

He was a tall skinny kid with very black hair that went over his eyes and ears and had bad teeth. He started laughing and teasing me that I had lost my way, which made the other kids all laugh. I felt very out of place and very nervous, at the same time one girl also from the higher grades came over also laughing at me, and she looked like she was coming for trouble. She too had long black hair that looked wild as if she didn't take care of it, not to mention having bad teeth herself. Both the girl and the kid looked very similar to each other, both tall and skinny with scruffy clothes as though they were brother and sister and they came straight over to me. – –

As soon as they approached me, they started shoving and pushing me around until I grew very angry, I then yelled out some obscenities to which the whole cafeteria overheard me. The older kids were very surprised to hear this from such a younger kid. With everyone staring at me as though I had two heads, I slowly went back to my table to finish my lunch, but that was just the beginning of a situation that would end up outside in the playground. – –

After lunch we all headed outside to the playground where I met up with my classmates, it felt so refreshing to getting back to my friends, especially going through the experience that I had with the older kids. Shortly after the tall kid along with the girl walked over to me and kept badgering me about why would I curse a girl out in the middle of the cafeteria, she then jumped in and started to do the same. After a few exchanges of words, she then started pushing me around.

As the pushing and shoving continued, I grew very angry then kicked her against her knee, as I did so I saw the expression on her face as if she was pretty hurt, she then went into a corner and said something to the kid, that is when he came over and stated that I shouldn't hit girls especially in that manner. After the incident I noticed that she walked away with a limp, I somehow felt sorry to what I had done to her, but being teased and bullied by these two I didn't have too much of a choice. After the whole incident they both walked away. It wasn't long before we would meet again but it would be in the mornings at the schoolyard.

It was about two days later when he came back looking for me, sometimes he would threaten to fight me, other times it would be just teasing and bullying around. This went on for a couple of days and every time he would come back looking for me, I would try to hide behind the other kids as to avoid him. At one time he saw me cowardly hiding behind some kids, suddenly he stared at me with those piercing black eyes then headed straight to me. At that same moment I thought I was dead, however he then did something that surprised me, he grabbed my shoulder and strangely started laughing, to my relief I would live again.

After that he suddenly lost interest and stopped coming around, I guess he found some other coward to bully around.

CHAPTER 3

STRANGER AT THE DOOR

Some of the most memorable moments that I would have would be right on my front porch, after all at an early age your mother wouldn't want you to venture off so far on your own. But sometimes things happen in the simplest places that you would never suspect, and in this case it would be right on my front porch.

Sitting on my porch I would meet with my friends where we would chat and make plans to go over to the park or just walking around the block to see what we could find to do. Sometimes we would go over to a friend who lived around the corner where he had the entire addict as a clubhouse, we later decided to make one for ourselves in my garage, which in the end wouldn't turn out too well.

One day while sitting on the porch it started to rain, after the rain had stopped my friends and I came together and took some wooden twigs or some ice cream sticks that we would find and run to the curb where the water would be running down the street like a little river. We would then place our sticks onto the water and watch them race down the street. It was times like this that taught me, you didn't need so much to enjoy yourself. –

Other times I would love spending my time reading some of my favorite comic books such as Tarzan and Conan the barbarian, but I also was very fond of reading books about the early pioneers and old Western novels on cowboys and Indians, stories of Daniel Boone, Davy Crockett and many other characters of early America which was very inspirational to me.

My friends and I along with my sisters would play all sorts of games, such as hide and seek and use the porch as a home base. We would enjoy many great times on my porch, whether it was with my sisters or with my friends, we shared many great and crazy experiences together.

However, there was one very strange experience on that porch where me and my sisters would never forget. My cousins were in town visiting and my parents had set up a party with a bunch of friends over that lasted throughout the night. The adults kept pretty much inside and as usual we found them to be boring, so we decided to go out to the porch. We stayed out all night joking around and telling each other stories until I heard a sound as if someone was moving around in the dark.

Now the sounds were coming from the backyard, but then moved slowly closer to the front where the porch was. I couldn't see who or what it was because it was so dark out. We then dared each other to see who would be brave enough to go over and see what it was making the strange sound, of course we all chickened out, but later that night is when something very strange happened.

Because of the creepy sounds coming from the backyard, we decided to go upstairs and play a few games. That is when my mother had asked my sister to bring down a pot of rolled up cabbage that she had made earlier for the party. As my sister headed downstairs with the pot, we all decided to go down together, that is when something very strange happened.

Now the stairway went straight down towards the front door, and being that it was summer time we only had the screen door shut, and that is when we all saw something standing at the front door, it was a tall person under some dirty sheets with its arms stretched out and waving around. There was no face, no hands nothing but a tall figure under some sheets waving at us with a large cane.

My sister yelling out in fear – dropping the pot, ran back upstairs with the rest of us behind her, not to mention watching the pot rolling down the stairs with the food all over the place.

Upon hearing the screams and all the commotion, my parents ran out to see what was going on, all confused and scared we told them what we saw, the rest of the adults were all pretty quiet regarding the situation which made us even more confused. Now none of the adults admitted being that figure and we never did find out who or what was it that night. –

CHAPTER 4

THE MOVIE NIGHT

One day all the kids at school were talking about a movie that was coming on TV, it was some sort of vampires from outer space sci-fi movie which I was a big fan of. I was very excited and couldn't wait to see it, however there was one problem, for some reason my television was not working at the time, now I knew that my friends next-door had a much better set, and I was very determined to see the movie, so I had to come up with something and fast.

Later that evening I told my mother that I would go out and sit on the porch for a while, as soon as I went out, I headed towards my friends next-door hoping that I would be able to watch the movie with them. So I went over where I explained to my friends mother about my situation. She told me that they were busy with dinner and that it was too late for company, now being a stubborn kid, I was determined to see the movie, so I pretended to leave and walked around the back. –

I then noticed a window behind the house, where I might be able to see the movie through the back window. Of course, they found out that I was poking through their window and it wasn't long before their mother came out. All confused she asked me what was I doing, I then explained to her about the whole situation and she felt a bit sorry for me, then asked if I would like to come in and watch the movie with them. I did get to see the movie however, before I could finish watching the rest of it, my mother was already at the door. –

CHAPTER 5

A SPECIAL FRIEND

There are times in life when something happens and the experience you go through would change your outlook in life forever, and it would always come unexpectedly.

Beginning at a very young age having good friends was very important to me, especially when you're going through tough times, or when you're feeling down, that is when you look to that someone who would always be there for you.

It was a warm and sunny afternoon and I was sitting on my porch, but for some reason I felt very down and lonely which never happened to me, because I always had my sisters and friends around. As I sat on my porch, I noticed a small dog sitting down in front of my yard watching me, I believe it was a beagle which is one of my favorite types of dogs. As I called him over his little tail started waggling, at first he was hesitant, but then he inched towards me and sat there staring at me as if he was waiting for something.

As he came closer, he seemed very friendly, he then began licking me all over my face, I grew very fond of him right away, so I took him onto my yard and played around with him for a while. He was very playful and looked like a puppy but a bit older. He would fetch the sticks that I would throw around and would bring it right back over to me. He stayed with me throughout the day, everywhere I would go he would follow, and when I stopped, he would sit and wait until I continued on.

It was now getting late and I wanted to bring him inside the house, however my mother did not trust him and stated that if the dog really likes you, he will wait for you throughout the night. I was very worried that he would leave, So I gave him some water and a hot dog just to make sure he wouldn't leave. My mother then put him out on the porch where he just sat there then curled up like a little ball in the corner.

I was very fond of this dog and worried that he would leave, I laid in bed and thought of him throughout the night. As the next day came, I ran over to see if he was still out on the porch, and to my surprise he was still there sitting in front waiting for me. I was very happy about the whole thing, I then decided to take a walk down the block with my new friend.

As we walked down the block, a neighbor of mine came over and started petting him, the dog then came straight back over to me and sat by my side. Right there and then I felt as if he were not only my dog but a close friend to me. As we continued down the block, I then went over to a field where I would go over to many times. At this field there were many chipmunks that I would always love watching and even try catching them, but the little critters were to fast for me. –

Here I would watch them peeking out through their burrows, then would run back in once I got to close, now with my little friend with me I introduced him to the chipmunks, in hoping that maybe with his help I would be able to catch one. As we got to the field he didn't hesitate to run around, I watched him go over to the burrows where he would try and dig a hole in order to get one of these little chipmunks.

I then looked around until I saw a chipmunk sitting on top of his burrow, I knelt down and started to crawl over towards him, at the same time the dog looked like he was inching over towards the borrow himself. As I got closer to the chipmunk, I jumped up and ran around trying to catch him. Chasing these little critters was fun, but there was no way we would be able to catch one. As I took a little rest from all the running around, I noticed my little friend was still trying to catch one on his own. It was so funny to see this little dog chasing them around, I had such a great time watching him in that field. –

The day was long and pretty hot, we both were tired and thirsty then strangely I saw a bottle of water that was laying nearby. I say this because my neighborhood was a pretty well-kept area and never had any trash laying around. I looked over to him and saw that he looked just as thirsty as I was, so I gave it over to him where he finished it pretty fast, after finishing up he came over to me and started licking my face again. –

As the day went on, we sat in the field enjoying the beautiful day, Suddenly a neighbor of mine who lived down the block saw me sitting in the field, he then came over and asked me if I was hungry and gave me a box of cracker jacks, it was the perfect timing because I was very hungry and I knew that my little friend was hungry as well.

We went over to a tree nearby and sat in the shade for some rest, I then shared the crackerjack box with him, as we ate together, I took out the little surprise that would come with the crackerjack box, this time it was a tiny comic in a plastic package.

As I started to read it, I noticed that he came over to me as though he wanted me to share the story with him, so I started reading it to him. Now I know it sounds silly but he actually sat there as if he was interested in the story, As I sat there reading, he then laid down next to me with his head on my lap, I was growing very fond of this little dog and felt as if he was a very special friend of mine.

He was a tiny little dog and very friendly who would always be by my side, to tell you the truth I have never felt such loyalty and friendship as I did with that little dog. I told myself that when I get back home, I would ask my mother if I could keep him. As the day went on, we ventured around the field looking for more chipmunks or anything else that might catch our interest. We then Started running around in circles like two crazy kids chasing each other, after all the running around, I was a little tired and went to sit down on the curb with my little friend sitting down next to me. –

Shortly after a stranger walked by with a very odd look on his face, as he came closer the dog began barking at him as though he was watching over me. For some reason it was the only time he had done this. Then the dog did something very strange, he came between me and the man and kept barking until the stranger left. After the incident the dog came back over to me and started licking me as though he was making sure I was all right. All I could remember was the man walking away staring back at us with a strange look on his face.

The day was long, both of us were tired and hungry so we started for home. As we walked back home, suddenly a street cleaner came by and the dog began barking and chasing after it, I tried holding him back but he kept going after it until I couldn't see him any longer. I tried following the truck but it went out to far, later I walked over to where the truck had gone off to and looked around for him, but he was nowhere to be seen. I went over to the curb and sat there waiting to see if he would return. –

After waiting for some time, I decided to go back over to the field where we had been earlier in hoping that he might have came back. I looked all over for him, but he was nowhere in sight. It was now getting late and I started towards home, walking back I felt very different, a sense of loss went through me, as if I had lost something very special to me, I felt very alone.

The next day I woke up and looked all around my yard, then asked my mother if she had saw him anywhere around the house but there was no luck. I then walked back to the field hoping that he might be there waiting for me, as I got there he was nowhere around. Then a feeling came over me, I felt as if I had lost something very special and dear to me, a sense of emptiness and confusion went through my head, even my body felt different, to me I have never felt that way before.

As I started back home, I saw some of my friends playing around, they looked over and asked me to join them, now normally I would run over, but for some reason I didn't feel the same and quietly walked away. My friends were all confused as to what was wrong, but to me I couldn't get that little dog out of my head, and that empty feeling inside.

The next day I decided to go back over to the field in hoping that he might be there waiting for me, I even took the little comic book from the crackerjack box with me as a crazy idea that if he was there, I would read it to him. As I approached the field, I saw some chipmunks running around but the dog was not there, it wasn't the same without him, I then started back home.

As I walked back home, a strange feeling went through me, that I would never see him again. I walked back over to my porch and sat down wondering what happened to my little friend and why did it have to happen. Everything felt very different from that moment on, after losing him I never felt the same again. It might sound strange but, to this day I have never felt the happiness and joyful feelings as I did when I was with him, the sense of friendship and loyalty which meant so much to me was now gone. I never did find out what happened to that little dog, I only knew him for a couple of days, but to me losing him was like losing a best friend who would always be there for you. —

CHAPTER 6

THE GREAT OUTDOORS

As a kid having good friends around you is probably one of the most important things in your life. But it is also true for when you venture away from home for the first time, whether it's for several hours or for several days, it is those memorable moments in your life that you find out just how lucky you are to have shared those moments.

My friends next door were three outgoing kids who were very avid hunters, they started at a very young age with their father. But It was through their father who would go hunting every other week or so that I got to learn a great deal about the outdoors. It was a typical deer Hunter seen, where he would drive up to the house with the deer on the hood, and other times it would be rabbits, ducks and of course fishing. It was at this time that I discovered the outdoors and found how much I loved it. We would go on camping trips and on certain occasions hunting, for me it was a great experience to see nature in the wild.

One morning however I was out playing around in my front yard, my friend from next door came out and told me that they were going frog hunting and he had put together a spear for spearfishing. Not only was he very excited to show me the spear, but just as determined to show me how good he knew how to use it. So confident in himself, he asked me to stand in position, so he can throw the spear between my feet. So convinced of his accuracy that he insisted that I stand in place. Of course, after his accurate throw, I had to pull out the spear from my foot and ran back home.

Curiosity always gets the best of a kid, and that's exactly what happened to me, when one day their father came back from a hunting trip. –

Every now and then their father would bring back something from hunting such as ducks, pheasants, rabbits and even some raccoons and squirrels. However, one day after bringing back some rabbits after hunting, he had skimmed them earlier and left them out to dry. His purposes, was to make some hats and other clothing features. I accidentally came across the rabbits and mistakenly took them for garbage, so I grabbed the skins and ran to my backyard where I had placed them on some wooden sticks.

My intention was to have the skins sewed together like a Daniel Boone hat, somehow my neighbors saw what I had done and came over with my mother, of course that didn't go too well. After that incident I believe that my neighbors asked my mother to have me committed.

My friends next door who were very experienced with the outdoors, showed me all kinds of ways on how to live outdoors, even how to build shelters and making traps for hunting. I would always admire their hunting skills, and would learn a lot from them, especially when we would get together on a trip.

It was on my first fishing trip that changed my life on how I saw the world. Now I have never gone fishing or anywhere for that matter before, but being so far from home for the first time and without my mother, it would be a very inspirational and memorable experience.

It was on that trip that I discovered just how much I loved the outdoors. We had gone away for a couple of days with my three friends and their father, now they were already experienced for the outdoors but to me it was a whole new world. We would wake up early in the morning and hike up to some trails leading to a lake, we would then put together our fishing gear and have a good time waiting for a bite. That was when I caught my first fish, now it might not sound so special but to a seven-year-old kid catching your own fish for the first time was a very special feeling for me, and I was very excited to have done so. We later sat down at our camp and placed our fish on some rocks, where they taught me all about cleaning and preparing the fish. –

Later that evening we set up our fire and began to prepare our meal, that was when I had a taste of the fish I caught earlier. Now I had eaten fish before, however catching and cooking your own meal out in the wilderness seemed very different, and that experience changed me on how I saw things from that day on. Later that night we put together some logs to sit on and started telling each other stories, and would have a few laughs. As the night went on, I saw an owl that was in a tree nearby, and of course we would hear him every now and then, along with the frogs and other critters that would come out at night. Looking up at the night sky I was amazed to see so many stars, I have never seen so many before, for me it was a magical moment in my life. Being outdoors for the first time was an amazing experience for me, I had learned a great deal, and those experiences would stay with me throughout my entire life.

CHAPTER 7

THE WHITE RABBIT

I would always love venturing outside, even if it was just around the corner or around the block, I would always look for some adventure. One day me and a friend of mine decided to walk around the block as we normally would, then I spotted a beautiful white rabbit to which we started chasing after it.

The rabbit ran into some bushes and somehow got stuck, I quickly reached over and pulled it out, by this time it looked very frightened, it was shaking to the thought that we might harm it in some way. I felt sorry for the rabbit from going through such an ordeal and decided to take it home with me.

As we got to my house, I quickly looked around for some boxes to make some sort of cage for it. After looking around, I asked my friend to look after the rabbit while I put something together. As I entered my house my mother asked me to do some chores, now I don't remember how long it was before I returned back to my friend, as I did so I noticed that he did not have the rabbit with him.

As I asked him where was the rabbit, he looked very confused and stated that some people who lived nearby had taken it away from him. As soon as he described to me who they were, I knew right away who it was.

They were strange people who lived on the other side of my house, I hated them because of their constant trespassing into my yard and grabbing my stuff, they were a nuisance and a menace to everyone on the block. My other neighbors had a dislike for them just as my mother did, she had numerous quarrels with their mother who looked like an overweight Gypsy.

Not only were they a nuisance to everyone, but they all looked very strange and ugly, I say this because of their two front teeth in the middle was sharpened just like a vampire bat would, and this was true for their entire family.

Angry and frustrated of what happened, I headed towards their house with my friend. As soon as we got there, I noticed something that disturbed me greatly, –

To my shock the rabbit was already killed, they already had started cutting it up and the head was already cut off, and it's fur was laid aside. This was very disturbing to me because it all happened so fast, especially in that short matter of time. I stood there in shock and anger, and to make matters even worse two of the kids were laughing at me as though they were taunting me. I then started yelling and cursing them, then began throwing some rocks at them including their mother who at this point was also laughing and yelling at me. –

As I screamed and cursed at them, my neighbors came out and was angered at what these people had done, at the same time this was going on, my mother had also heard me yelling and came over to see what was all the commotion about. As she learned of what happened, she to yelled and cursed them, not only because of the rabbit, but because of their nuisance, that hatred and anger stayed with me for quite some time.

I later had some friends of mine come over and explained the situation to them. That night we hid behind some bushes, where we grabbed a bunch of rocks then started throwing them against their windows. It wouldn't bring back my rabbit but the anger was too much, and smashing their windows and watching them all confused and frightened made me feel much better. To my delight I later learned that they had moved away a week later – was it because of me or that the whole neighborhood hated them – I really didn't care.

CHAPTER 8

THE HILL

Having your first bicycle is always a special moment, even when things don't go according to plan.

I was about seven years old when my mother finally got me one, after all I was constantly badgering her about getting one for me. One day she decided to go out and get one, however I didn't know anything about it until she came back later that day. She had arranged for her friend to come over and babysit me while she was out, after a while I saw her come back with a cab, as he pulled up to the house, the driver walked over to the trunk and pulled out a bicycle. As you can imagine I was so excited to see that bicycle, to me it meant everything a kid could want, so I ran straight to it and jumped right on.

My friends had gathered around to see my new bike, I was just as excited to show it off, now I didn't even know how to ride a bicycle at the time, but because I was so excited, I jumped on without realizing how to ride. My friends were trying to teach me all about riding, but the thrill of me riding my own bicycle was too much, so I jumped on and started off on my own. Down the block I rode but because of all the excitement, I didn't even know how to stop, I kept going until I came across an old woman's tomato garden and the only way to stop was to smash through everything in my way. –

Smashing through the tomato garden wasn't the worst thing, to my luck the old woman was standing there watching the whole thing.

Suddenly I saw her running towards me yelling with her broom, as soon as I saw this crazy old women chasing me, I dropped my bike and ran back down the street straight to my mother. She then stopped the woman from trying to hit me and of course there were arguments. As for me I was not able to ride my bike for about a week later.

Afterwards when I got my bicycle back, I would ride around with my friends always looking for some fun and a little mischief, and sometimes we got more than what we bargained for, such as the time when we rode around thinking we were the big boys on the block and came across some girls on their bikes. –

Now the girls were about 14 years old, nonetheless, we yelled out to them how pretty they were, and if they would like to come over and hang out with us. Suddenly the girls turned around and headed straight for us. As soon as we saw them heading over, our hearts like our confidence suddenly dropped, all confused and nervous, we didn't even know what to say. As soon as they rode up and knowing that we were little young brats, they decided to make an example out of us.

Right away the girls started with their questioning, and of course the first question was how old were we, and what kind of tricks were we able to do. The only answer we could come up with was that we could go pretty fast – the girls laughing then stated that they will teach us some new tricks.

Suddenly one of the girls even rode down the street with one wheel up in the air, then the other girl rode down the street standing on her seat. After watching these girls performing their skills, we left in a hurry like pathetic little nerds, all embarrassed and humiliated, we retreated back to reality.

We then headed towards the neighborhood park where we could find some way to redeem ourselves or at least a way to find our dignity again. –

The community park was several blocks from the house, and it was where many of the kids in the neighborhood would go over to. My sisters along with my friends would go swimming in the pool, sometimes have a baseball game or just fool around with the other kids, there was also the dirt bike paths, where many of the experienced kids took their bikes and would ride up and down these rough and crazy terrains. But then there was the infamous Hill where many of the kids would prove their bravery as well as having an adventure for a lifetime. –

As every kid growing up, you would come across challenges, and sometimes you would have to face those challenges willingly or not. It was at the hill where I would find my challenge, and it was here where you would prove to yourself just how brave or stupid you really were. The hill was the major focus point for most of the kids especially the boys, we would take our bikes over to the top of the hill, and once at the top we would dare each other to ride down as fast as possible.

Now this was no ordinary hill, there was a meandering path going all the way down with menacing jagged rocks protruding out on each side of the path. The kids would meet at the hill to watch the daredevils riding their bikes up and down the rough terrain which was adjacent to the hill.

The whole purpose of this was to see, who would be more daring and brave enough to ride down the hill full speed without falling off, and of course live to tell about it. –

Now there would be three categories of kids, the veterans who had battle scars from their encounter with the rough terrain, then you had the first timers such as myself out to prove something, and the spectators. Any kid who wanted to take the ride down this terrain, would have to climb up the hill with their bikes, once there you would wait your turn to be the next one going down.

Now the story was that once at the top, you would start shaking, some would start crying to get off and others would look down the hill grabbing their handlebars with white knuckles, rethinking the whole idea. But whatever the case as for me the time had come, it was now my turn. –

Once at the top, you could hear all the other kids cheering you on, I felt like I was a daredevil such as evil Knievel waiting to impress the crowd down below. Standing at the top of the hill you felt like you were special as well as invincible. I was now at the top and ready to take that terror ride downhill. – – –

As I got closer to the edge, I looked down the path of the hill and all I could see was how steep the path really was, not to mention the jagged stones protruding out at both sides. Suddenly all of the euphoria that I had built up before, dropped like my heart did. Then reality steps in, your heart is pounding, you become nervous and don't know if you should continue, but the cheering from the kids down below helps to motivate you, and gives you that extra courage to carry on. I inch my bicycle forwards to the edge of the hill, with the wind blowing in my face, I then back up to get a running start and suddenly I storm down.

Going down was not what I had thought, it was worse! – –

As your bike tilts downwards, you realize just how high you are, and how menacing the hill really is. Suddenly your bike picks up speed and you are now in freefall, as your bike rushes downwards you try to avoid the jagged rocks that are on both sides, suddenly as you are racing downwards you come to realization that there is no stopping and you have absolutely no control of the situation – you are now at the mercy of the hill – which has none.

Racing down the hill, you're bouncing around like a rag doll with no control of the matter, you then grab on to your bike for dear life, hoping that you are not thrown against the jagged rocks below. You're waiting for this terror ride to end – but it doesn't, the ride downhill now seems like it goes on forever and there's no way of stopping. Then to your surprise, you see the ground coming up ahead and hope that you are lucky enough to hit the ground in one piece, you tighten your grip on your handlebars and brace for impact. –

Once you hit bottom, your bicycle slams against the ground and you are then thrown against your handlebars, smashing your chest against the cold hard steel. Afterwards you fall to the ground, all dizzy and out of breath, you lay down on the floor holding your bruised chest and try making sense of what just happened.

After the terror ride, you pick up your bike and brush off all the dirt, as you do a feeling of relief sets in that the worst is finally over, then something comes across you, a feeling of accomplishment flows through, knowing that not only have you survived the hill, but you have beaten that inner fear and overcame your challenge.

Then you are met with kids patting you on the back as though you are their hero. There was a tree nearby where the kids would etch the names of those who had made it down the hill, and to have your name on the list made you feel very special, a sense of pride goes through you that only a seven-year-old could dream of.

With the sun going down and all bruised up, I pick up my bike and gather with my friends, who like me had enough of the day. I then throw a towel over my shoulder and drink some much needed, cold soda to quench my thirst. We then tell each other about our experiences laughing all our bruises away and with a memory of a lifetime we head for home.

CHAPTER 9

BALLOONS FOR STITCHES

Growing up with my sisters I had quite a few feuds with them, especially my oldest sister who resembled more of a – tom boy. She was always quick to join me and my friends in wherever we would go, and would have many of the same interests that the boys would, such as bike riding, playing baseball and climbing hills.

As for me and my sister sharing, that was another story, at one time we had a party over the house with some ice cream cake, now there were lots of kids over and there was not enough cake to go around. With my sister seeing that there were no more left, she had threatened me to hand over my cake to her, as usual I said no, a minute later she had smashed my head against the refrigerator. This of course led to a gaping gash right over my eyes.

With blood all over the place, my mother rushed me over to the hospital where they had stitched me up, before coming home the nurses had given me several balloons. Shortly after coming home, my sister came over to me and threatened to hit me over the head if I didn't give her a balloon. Once again I refused to do so, she then grabbed a broomstick and smashed it across my head – opening up the stitches.

Let's just say I had to run back to the hospital so they could stitch me up again. –

CHAPTER 1∅

THE GARAGE

There was a garage at the very back of the house that was rarely used, it was pretty much kept empty. One day my sister and I asked my mother if we could clean it out and make it into a clubhouse, after all it was barely used for anything at all. My mother agreed, so we started to arrange our clubhouse with old chairs, tables and anything else that we came across.

However, we later found out that there was a beehive inside the garage walls. Now there were two openings, one on the inside and the other on the outside. At first we had no problems with them, but that all later changed, they began to become a nuisance, so much so that we couldn't use the garage anymore. That is when we decided to do something about it, we later got together with our friends and planned to go to war against them.

The bees soon began flying all over the garage inside and out, not only did they take over the garage but now they were swarming outside as well.

The backyard had many fruit trees, such as apples and peer trees, so I stated to everyone to grab as many apples and throw them against the opening of the hive. Reason for doing this was to block the hive or at least, stop them from coming out. After a while of doing this, it not only didn't help with the matter, but now made everything worse.

Not only were the bees even more angry, but now they started flying out in droves and coming for us. The next thing to do was to make some torches out of paper bags and sticks, once again, the fire just made the bees more aggressive and now were stinging us left and right. One of my friends was stung in the eye, both of my sisters were stung as well, one on the butt and on my other sister I noticed that there were two bees tangled

27

in her hair, I quickly picked up a stick and slammed it across her head hoping to hit the bees.

However, I don't think I hit any.

As the fighting continued, my cousin grabbed a torch and poured extra fluid on it, he then started waving the stick around and over his head until he to was stung right in the eye. At the same time he was stung, he dropped the burning bag against his chest, luckily for him he was not hurt bad but had a great swollen eye. And yes, I was also a casualty of the bee war, being stung twice one on my arm and the other on my ankle.

Later the bees became too much it was now a swarm, our parents noticed this and rushed out to help with the matter, but to no avail the bees were too much. We accepted defeat and retreated back with our parents running behind us. Later the neighbors had called the fire department to hose down the bees. With all of us having been stung, some more than others we all developed a greater respect and understanding for the bees.

Chapter II

THE FIRE

Behind our backyard there was a great large field of grass and some trees here and there, me and my friends would go over to this field many times. One day my mother and two other women was raking some grass together, I believe they were cleaning out the area to make a garden. Now my mother already had done some gardening in our yard, but on this day for some reason she started clearing out an area to grow some vegetables. Then one of my cousins had found a dead bird and spilled some lighter fluid over the bird, as he did so he put a box over the bird and lit it on fire. –

Upon seeing smoke coming from the box, and being curious misfits that we were, we kicked the box over to see the bird on fire, suddenly the fire spread out so fast against the dry grass. This fire had spread out so fast that now we were caught up in the middle of it. It looked like it had formed a circle around us, my mother ran out quickly grabbing my sisters while yelling for the rest of us to leave.

— —

At the same time all this was going on, I had a strange experience that I cannot explain. The fire had spread so fast all around the field, then looked as if it had encircled me. Now I was not one to panic however I did get pretty nervous and tried looking for a way to get out of there, but because of all the commotion I could not see any way out. –

At the same time this was going on, a strange incident happened, suddenly I saw some bright lights all around me and felt as if I was in a bubble. I couldn't hear anything and a feeling came over me that nothing would hurt me. A sense of comfort and peace went through me, telling me that I would be all right and nothing would happen to me. –

Then something pointed my attention to the beautiful blue skies overhead, that is when I noticed a bright light that encircled me, suddenly everything seemed so quiet and very peaceful. As I looked back to see what was going on, I saw my mother yelling and trying to put out the fire, some neighbors were there to help. But as I looked around, I noticed that everyone moved as though they were in slow motion. Confused and unaware of what was going on, I stood there not in fear, but in comfort and peace, that everything would be all right. –

Suddenly I found myself in a different area, this time outside of the fire zone. As for me I cannot explain what had happened, nor how I got to be on the other side. My mother was just as surprised and quickly pulled me out of the way. Then a friend of mine who had been at the field, asked me where did I go, at first I didn't understand what he meant, but from what he told me is that, they couldn't see me in that field. I don't know how long this whole situation lasted, and I cannot explain it. Shortly after the fire department was already running over to put out the fire. I never did tell anyone about this experience until now, but that moment stayed with me for the rest of my life. –

CHAPTER 12

MY SLINGSH⊕T

There was an alleyway behind my house that looked like it went on forever, we would run up and down this alleyway many times, and it was here that I carved out my first slingshot. Now we were always making all types of gadgets with our pocket knives which we constantly carried around. One day we had carved out some sticks to make a bow and arrow, now my friends and I would make these often, however he then decided to show me how to carve out my first slingshot.

As we gathered our sticks, we later got some rubber from the store and strapped on the rubber bands to the sticks. After putting the slingshots together, we ventured off down the alley until we came across a box. Now it looked like it was someone's garbage that was thrown out, however upon looking inside I found several cartridges of bullets in which we were all very excited to see. We each took some cartridges and stuffed them in our pockets, later we went around looking for some cats or other targets to test our new slingshots. –

As we continued down the alley, suddenly out of nowhere a man came running after us shouting that we had gone into his garage and was stealing his items. He then he grabbed one of my friends and kept shouting at us and that he would call the police on my friend.

All shocked and confused as to what was going on, we tried explaining to the man as to what was going on, and that we haven't taken anything. However, he kept insisting that we had gone into his garage and would take us to the police. At this point we didn't know what to do, and my friend who the man was holding onto kept yelling to be let go. Our shock and confusion then turned to anger, then my friends brother started shooting the man with the slingshots and yelling at him, to let go of his brother.

At this point we all started shooting the man with our slingshots, to which he finally let my friend go, however he was very angered at us shooting him with the slingshots. We then picked up everything and ran as fast as possible, as we did so I heard my friends laughing and finally realized that, they did go into his garage earlier that day. I kind of brushed it off because the situation was already over and I couldn't change what happened. But to tell you the truth, it felt pretty good to use the slingshots to get away in a situation as the one we encountered.

As we continued walking down the alley, we would shoot at most anything we saw, whether it was a telephone pole, some cans and even at some cats that would venture nearby. Then to the corner of my eye I saw a bird just sitting on a branch, I took out my slingshot as fast as I can and shot straight at him. – –

Without even aiming at him I had accidentally killed him on the spot, my friends were all surprised to see what had happened, and wondered how could I have hit that bird so fast with one shot. I was just as surprised and speechless myself, then my friends did something which I have never seen them do before, they dug a hole and put the bird inside. I later asked them what was the reason, they stared back at me and stated that, it was a sin to kill for no reason.

I was surprised to hear this from these guys, after all they were the ones who were always going hunting and killing all kinds of creatures. After explaining to me that when they would go hunting, it was for food and not just some random killing, I now had a better understanding and respect of the whole idea of hunting. –

As we walked back home, I couldn't wait to show my mother the slingshot that I had put together, I felt it as a sense of a personal achievement that I had put together. After that day I would take my slingshot most anywhere I would go, and it was for two main reasons, the first was to have it with me as a constant reminder that I had made it all on my own, and of course to show it off to my other friends.

CHAPTER 13

VENTURING INTO THE UNKNOWN

The field behind the house was very large and vast, no homes, nothing but a great big empty field in which we had many fun times going into. Sometimes I would venture inside with my sisters, other times it would be with my friends. One day we decided to see what was on the other side of the field, so we got together and ventured out like explorers into the unknown. – –

We grabbed some sticks because we never knew what was awaiting us, so we took our sticks with us as our only defense against whatever lay beyond the field. It was a hot sunny day and we had walked quite a while before we came up to a moat. Now the moat was put there by workers to keep kids away from crossing over, however being inquisitive kids that didn't stop us at all, we simply put a board across the moat like a bridge then crossed over.

After crossing over we experienced some difficulties, there was some sort of mud all over the ground which made it harder to walk through. However, as we ventured further the ground became more solid and was much easier to walk across. further into the field we came across some trees and took a rest against them from the hot sun, one of my cousins tried climbing the trees to see if he could see what laid behind, we then found out there was an opening on the other side.

As we went further into the field, we saw large gravel mounds, at first some of the mounds were of smaller size rocks and pebbles, but then they became larger as we went further inside. We kept going until we finally got into a quarry, the mounds of gravel were of various types, some were small rocks others looked like coal, but many were of different colored dirt such as iron deposits and other minerals. As we continued walking across these hills of gravel and dirt, the larger they became. At first climbing these mounds were not so easy, many times our feet would sink into them, not to mention the small stones that would fill into our shoes every step we took. Later the mounds became harder and more compact which made it much easier to climb. –

We then came across mounds that looked like mountains. Some of these dirt mounds were so large that giant dump trucks would go up and down these mounds in a circle like a layer cake, traveling upwards to dump their load, then would come back down again. I loved playing on these mounds, we would play for hours watching these trucks go back and forth, not to mention playing on the mounds themselves.

The purpose of the gravel and other minerals was to be used by the Ford factory which was nearby, and would be hauled off by railroad. Now there weren't just one rail line of trains, they were more like four lines, and they would go back and forth to the factory on a daily basis. There were many times where we had climbed onto these trains, sometimes they were stationary and other times moving, in one case as we were playing on one, it suddenly started off.

At first we were too scared to jump off, but then the fear turned to excitement and stayed on to see where it would go. The train kept going until it approached a loading facility where it had finally slowed down, that gave us enough time to get off before we found ourselves who knows where. –

Shortly after we decided to go over to the quarry's main distribution center, where they would crumble the gravel together and would load them up on to the trains. We somehow managed to get inside without being seen, and that's when I saw what looked like giant buckets of gravel being moved around and onto the conveyor belts, the gravel was being distributed to different locations of the quarry. It was almost impossible to hear one another because of all the noise coming from the conveyor belts, and the machinery that were all over the place, not to mention the giant dump trucks that were all around the area transporting tons of gravel and minerals. – –

Later we decided to go over to a different site at the quarry, however that is when we would come across a sticky situation. As we continued to walk across the quarry, there were some areas that looked like wet clay, so we tried to walk across this area to get to the other side not knowing the consequences.

Walking the grounds of the quarry, there would be large pools of water on the ground that resembled a small pond and wet clay. Because of our curiosity, we decided to walk across this, wet clay to see how it would hold up and as we found out not too well. Once you stepped onto this clay there was great difficulty in getting out, and pulling your foot out meant your shoe would stay behind. – –

At one point I tripped and fell into this pool of clay and suddenly my arms were halfway in. As I tried pulling myself out, my foot got stuck and the more I tried to pull out, the further down my feet would sink in. It was as though you were in quicksand, the more I tried to get out, the more I would sink in.

My feet sank up to my ankles, and probably would have gone further if I didn't pull out. The same thing happened to my friends, some worse than others, but we eventually got out of the area and onto hard dry ground. –

After getting out of the mud trap, we all sat around laughing at our situation. It was now late evening and we all looked like we had a mud wrestling match. By this time the Clay had hardened all over our clothing, on some of us you couldn't tell what color clothing we had on. The time was now getting late, all muddy and dirty we headed for home.

The times and memories that I had at that quarry would stay with me throughout my years, I wouldn't have traded that place for any playground in the world. –

CHAPTER 14

THE FOOTBALL TEAM

At my school we had kids of various ages, which went from kindergarten up to fifth graders, with the older kids on the higher floors and the younger ones on the lower floors. However, there was a football team that I would see throughout the day. Walking to school in the mornings I would see them all gathered together before class, after school they would have their uniforms on practicing their game.

Watching the players with their uniforms on, and having all the attention was very impressive to me. I always admired them because of their status at the school, being the older kids and with their teammates all wearing their colorful jackets was very cool to see. Many of the younger kids such as myself, would look up to them as being some sort of role models. However, the players were not the only ones that I would admire, starting at a very young age me along with my friends had a big liking to the cheerleaders at the school, who would be around the players most of the time. With the colorful uniforms and having all the attention from the younger kids, especially the cheerleaders, was all the more reason for me to become one of them.

There were many times we would watch the cheerleaders practicing their cheers, and we would have a competition as to, who would go up to the girls and talk to them. Of course, none of us had the courage to do so, until one day a situation occurred. – –

One day after school, my friends and I decided to walk over to the football field where the team was practicing, we were very curious to see how they would go about doing so. Watching the players on how they supported one another was very inspiring for me, especially watching the quarterback, who to me resembled some sort of leader or general that I would always admire. The leadership role that he played taught me some valuable lessons for when I got older.

After watching them for a while, we then decided to walk over and see how it would feel to be part of the team. As we approached the players, I told them that we were big fans of the team and asked if we could try on the helmets. The team players thinking this was hilarious, handed us some helmets to try on, as I grabbed one, I realized that they were much larger and heavier than I had realized. Having the helmet on my head felt like I had a bucket over my head, which kept wobbling back and forth. Then I noticed some cheerleaders standing nearby, so we decided to go over and show off.

As we approached the girls, jokingly we stated to them that we were the new players on the team, to which they took this very amusingly and had a ball of the whole situation. Then one of the girls asked us which position do we play, now I didn't know anything about football except that they had uniforms and a ball, however my friend stated that we were in the second grade.

Let's just say this was hilarious, to both the girls and the teammates. Imagine a couple of seven-year-olds, trying to talk to and impress some fifth grade cheerleaders with your helmets wobbling back and forth. I didn't realize it at the time, but as I look back now it was hilarious.

But that little moment that we had with the team, made me realize something very important and I believe it was a valuable lesson to me later in life – and that is – you have to be somebody in order to get something out of life.

CHAPTER 15

THE ABAND⊕NED H⊕USE

As kids you're always curious of the world around you, and sometimes your curiosity would put you in situations that you wouldn't normally find yourself in.

At one time there was an abandoned house across the street from the school, this house was so torn up there were walls missing and obviously no doors and windows. So as you can imagine, a bunch of curious eight-year-old kids going across to this house for a little exploration and getting a little more than they bargained for. After school we would run over to see what we can find, to me it was more out of curiosity than anything else. I remembered the stairs going up to the second floor, and once I was up there, I could see my friends looking up at me from a great gapping hole on the first floor beneath me.

As we played around, we heard some strange sounds coming from one of the rooms upstairs, now I didn't know if it was from other kids but it was a creepy sound as if someone was banging on the wall, as soon as we heard this we started out the door as fast as possible. We returned to the house a couple of days later, and we would do so especially after school, now with our imaginations running wild we would dare each other to see who would be brave enough to go inside. Later it became a sort of playground for other kids who came by after school, there we would all meet and play all around the house. One day a bunch of older kids gathered together with us, and said that they would like to make it into a clubhouse. – –

We all agreed however, the older kids would be in control and would dictate as to how to organize our clubhouse. One of the older kids had started bullying one of my friends, then there was a shouting match in which my friend ended up with a black eye. Now I tried helping him out, only to realize I also came home with a black eye. –

After that incident, the older kids allowed us back into the house and accepted us as part of their group. Now this made me feel very special, knowing that you were a part of a group of your own made you feel very important.

However, this did not last long, they later closed down the house after one kid was hurt falling through one of the open floors.

CHAPTER 16

THE ⊕LD WITCH

◗ ● ◖

The abandoned house was not the only time we had ran into something that was a little creepy or strange, I remember one day some parents on the block were telling the kids in the area to be careful of an old woman who was supposedly a witch and lived a block or two down the road.

Now this was on the same route I would take going to school, I did not think of anything about this until one day me and a friend of mine going to school came upon the house, it was a very old and dirty place which looked round down and gave it that spooky look. With all kinds of garbage in the front yard such as old bicycle rims, tires and a bunch of boxes all scattered around the front of the house. And of course there were many cats around the house, some in the yard others sitting in front of the window. What made it even more strange was that the Windows seemed to be so dirty and cluttered around the edges that they looked like they never were opened.

We would pass the house many times going to school thinking nothing about it, until one morning when we saw the old woman coming out of the house. As she came out, her appearance resembled that of an old witch, I could see that she was wearing what looked like a long dirty old sweater with many layers, she also had long dirty gray hair that looked very wild and uncared for.

Then to my surprise my friend yelled out to her, she then looked and stared straight at us with a strange expression on her face. For a moment I thought she might come down running after us, but she looked very old and couldn't walk so fast. She then went back into the house as though she was kicking things around and went back inside, so we kept on our way to school. –

After school we would usually take different routes or shortcuts back home, but this time after hearing the stories about the old woman and the house, me and some friends decided to go down to the house to do some mischief. Such as throwing rocks into the Windows, as we walked down towards the house, I noticed some large plastic bags up against a tree near the house, at first I thought it was some garbage bags However, as we got closer we were shocked to see bloodstains around the bags, as well as what looked like the hooves of a sheep. –

To tell you the truth we were all more curious than scared to see what was inside, as we opened the bags, that is when I saw the head of a sheep that was skinned and with its eyes still in its sockets.

We all looked at each other in shock then confusion, I wondered who could have put this here and why, as we went through the bags the more parts we found. For some reason the site of the dead sheep did not scare us as much as the old woman did. Especially her house, which looked far more creepier than any dead sheep.

Suddenly we saw some people coming towards us, yelling to get away from the bags, we ran off not knowing what was going on and why was the sheep killed. After that incident we never did go near the old house, only to pass the house from across the street. –

CHAPTER 17

THE NICKELODEON

Going to school every morning I would take my usual route, once at school my friends and I would all meet at the playground before going to class. Here we would discuss the things we had done the day before, afterwards the bell would ring and we would all line up with our classmates and get ready for class.

Now every kid would always love it when Friday's would come along, however in this case the next best day was Wednesday. –

Every Wednesday after school there would be a movie night, and it would be held at the auditorium. One day my cousin and I decided to see a movie together, however to see the movie you would need a nickel to get in. As you enter the auditorium, you would stand on line and there would be a girl holding a box where you would drop your nickels into, then you would enter to watch the movie.

Now on this day we were very excited to see the movie however, I didn't have any nickels with me nor did my cousin, so I came up with a plan. I told him as he got closer to the girl – pretend to put a nickel into the box. So now were online and I'm in front of him and there were a couple of students in front of me, then I notice that the girl was watching very closely as to who had a nickel, that made me very nervous. As my turn came up, I walked over to her and pretended to put a nickel in the box, suddenly the girl stared at me – now this was for a few seconds – but felt like several minutes. I froze with my arm stretched out towards the box, then to my luck a teacher came over to the girl to discuss some matters – I quickly picked up a nickel from the box and threw it back in. – –

Then the girl looked at me as though she knew something was wrong, however she let me through because she could not prove whether I did or didn't have a nickel. It was another story for my cousin, he actually froze and didn't know what to do. Now we stood there for a few seconds but it felt like forever, I then told her that I had put in two nickels for the both of us, she now looked at me with discontent and didn't know what to believe, we stood there arguing about the situation, but because of the other students behind me she let us through anyway.

I can't tell you how nervous I was and how close we came from being caught, but we eventually got to see our movie. I remembered the movie being the jungle book, and I believe it was the very first jungle book movie made not the cartoon. It wasn't the best movie but when a situation occurs such as this one you would always remember it. –

Chapter 18

COMING HOME FROM SCHOOL

◦ ● ◦

Going to school in the mornings would be more of a normal routine however, coming back home was a different experience altogether. Sometimes my friends and I would take shortcuts through the neighbors backyard, while doing so we would have some crazy experiences along the way.

Now having strange kids running through your backyard wasn't the worst thing that could happen, however some neighbors took it that way, some would come out chasing us, others would come out yelling and screaming. However, there was one woman who I guess got to know our routine and was waiting there with the water hose.

One day as we were running through some backyards, we came across a house which had some ducks in the yard. As we went through, I thought of grabbing one to take home with me. I chased after him but he was pretty fast, he then started quacking which brought attention to the owner of the house. – – – –

Suddenly a woman came out yelling at me to leave the ducks alone, all nervous and confused I ran out as fast as possible and headed towards her fence to jump over it, however as I did so my shoes got caught on top, suddenly I tripped and laid there upside down. The woman seeing this thought that I was hurt, then yelled out – are you all right and came straight for me – at this point I didn't know if she was sincere or not, I started running and without looking slammed into her garbage cans. By this time the woman probably thought that I had some mental problems. –

Shortly after that incident we came across a very unusual situation, my friend who was still with me noticed an abandoned school with one of the main doors opened. –

I later noticed there was a book bag with a sweater against the door, we both looked at each other as to who did it belong to. We yelled out to see if someone would respond or come out of the building. Then we heard sounds coming from inside the building, we both looked at each other and asked which one of us would go inside. Suddenly there was a loud sound coming from inside, I was not sure if the sounds were made on purpose but we left in a hurry. –

CHAPTER 19

THE ST⊕Rɱ

In school we would have fire drills but also tornado drills as well, unlike a fire, on a tornado drill we would leave the classroom and go down to the first floor, there we would crouch down facing the wall with our hands behind our head. Now tornadoes were never a problem until one day one happened to pay a visit. I was at home playing around the front yard, it was a regular day and everything seemed pretty normal, that is until I noticed the neighbors all looking up and pointing to the skies.

I then saw my neighbor from next door running out of the house and telling everyone to get inside, at first I didn't understand what he was talking about, then I saw some dark clouds forming overhead, suddenly I saw the tail of the tornado coming down. Now I have never seen a tornado before and didn't understand what was going on, but to me it was very exciting to see a tornado being formed in front of your eyes. I looked up and saw the tale of the tornado getting longer as it came down, suddenly all I heard was the neighbors yelling to get inside and to the basement. –

That is when my mother grabbed me and my sisters then ran down into the basement, we then went into a room that was very different from the rest of the basement, it looked like some sort of bunker with cement blocks for walls and a pretty heavy door, I have never knew about this room until that day.

Then as the winds picked up, we all just waited for the storm to pass. All I could hear was the sound of strong winds and the crackling of trees being torn apart. –

The storm lasted for a very short time, after the winds had died down everything seemed so quiet, shortly after everyone started coming out and looking around to see of any damages.

Now right after this storm, you would think that we would have been more frightened of the whole ordeal, on the contrary as for me it was very exciting to go through such an experience. Shortly after the storm my friends and I had gathered together to venture out to see what had happened.

As we came out, I saw that the streets were littered with tree branches as well as garbage cans and everything else that the wind could toss around.

—

Later we heard a fire truck racing by, it stopped around the block and that is when we decided to chase after it to see what was going on. As we ran around the block, we notice that someone's garage was hit. There were a few damages afflicted on the garage by the tornado, parts of the garage was ripped apart and tossed all over the place. At the same time, we were too busy looking around for anything we might find, then to our surprise we spotted a rainbow, and to tell you the truth this rainbow was not only so beautiful, but looked like it was right around the corner.

And being the gullible kids that we were, we ran around the block trying to see if we could find the rainbow, of course the purpose was to find the pot of gold. As usual not only did we not find the rainbow, but there were no pot of gold there either.

After the storm my mother was cleaning up around the yard as was the rest of the neighbors, later I remembered the room in the basement that we had ran into, it was filled with jars of fermented foods of various types as well as salted cured meats. My mother was always putting things together, but I never did know where she would put the stuff until I had went into that room.

Later however, I would come across a disturbing situation as to what my parents would use this room for.

CHAPTER 20

THE SECRET ROOM

It was about a couple of weeks after the storm, I came home from school and noticed two kittens in my living room. I was very excited to see them and asked my mother, where did she get them from. She told me that she found them lurking around the yard just after the storm. –

Now I did have some cats around the house but didn't know they had babies, however this would not be the first time I would have some animals over as a surprise. –

As it happened, one day I was playing in the front yard and saw two of my father's friends come out of a van along with a sheep. As you can imagine I was very surprised to see this, not only to see a sheep, but what was the purpose of bringing one over, at this point I was confused but nonetheless very excited to have one. I asked my mother what was the sheep for, she looked at me as if she tried hiding something, then told me in a funny way that, we would have him as a pet for a while.

Later I saw my mother tying the sheep around a tree so he wouldn't run away, I told her that I would build a fence around him, and later asked if I could keep him as a pet. She stated that if I wanted to keep it, I would have to take care of him. Of course, I agreed and thought it would be fun to have a sheep as a pet, so I quickly started gathering some grass for him and looked around for sticks to make a makeshift fence. As I did so I remembered about the rabbit that I had lost to the people who used to live next door. So I looked around for the biggest sticks that I could find along with some rope, then tied them together around some trees, It resembled a makeshift stable and my mother was very impressed of what I had done.

The day went by pretty fast and it was now beginning to get dark, before going to bed I asked my mother if she would watch over the sheep while I would sleep, she laughed and stated that she would watch over him all night. Of course, I kept peeking out the window from time to time, until I finally fell asleep.

As morning came around, I quickly ran out to see if the sheep was still there, to tell you the truth I was very relieved to see him still there. The feeling of losing the rabbit was still fresh in my mind and was unsure of what would happen if I wasn't around. As the day went on, I was very excited to finish building my stable, then I asked my mother if I could have my friends over to see the sheep, suddenly she looked very nervous and told me not to tell anyone about it. I was very confused as to why. Nonetheless I ran over and told my friends, soon enough they were over to see the sheep and asked me where did I get it from. We later got together and started finishing up with the stable, and joked around that we should get a little farm going. –

Later that evening I saw some of my father's friends come over, now they would come over quite often, but this time there were more of them than usual. They stayed around pretty much throughout the night chatting like they always would. I then noticed that my mother looked very frigidity, she then asked me to go to bed. Later that night I was awakened by some strange sounds, I got out of bed and quietly looked to what was going on. I noticed it was my father's friends who was still there, however they were going up and down the stairs leading to the basement. Then I noticed that they were dragging a large bag downstairs, all confused of what was going on, tired and exhausted I fell back to sleep. –

As morning came, I headed outside where I noticed that the sheep was nowhere around, I asked my sister to help me look around for him. I was pretty nervous and thought that someone might have stolen him during the night, I quickly ran over to my mother and asked her about the sheep, she told me that the men had taken him away to a farm early this morning. As she told me this, I noticed that she had a very suspicious look on her face, I felt very uncomfortable with her answer. My sister and I went around the house looking for the sheep that was nowhere to be seen.

As we continued looking, we noticed the door leading to the basement was opened and decided to go downstairs. Now we rarely had gone downstairs on our own, for one reason it looked pretty scary, second my mother would always work on some fermented foods that she would put together, and wouldn't allow us downstairs. As we looked around the basement, my sister pointed to the corner and saw what looked like a blanket of wool, I then saw some blood stains around the floor and on the wool itself. Upon seeing this we felt that something was terribly wrong, but we continued anyway. We then saw the door to the room where my mother kept the salted meats, and it was wide open.

As we entered, I saw the sheep hanging on a hook from the ceiling, it was a shock to me looking at him hanging there, but then I was very angered, not only as to what had happened, but angry that my mother had lied to me about taking care of the sheep. Of course the whole idea of killing the sheep was for a holiday and for food, but I never did gain trust for anyone after that incident, especially adults.

CHAPTER 21

THE BLACK CAR

As a kid you grow up thinking that you know the world around you, you're especially gullible in believing whatever adults tell you even from strangers, such as the day when me and my sister found out just how gullible we can be –

once in a while my sisters and I would go across the street to a woman who we called grandma, she had a swing set in her backyard in which she would always invite us to come over and play with. she would bring over some-baked pies and cookies which were very delicious. I guess having kids over, made the old women feel more comfortable and useful instead of sitting at home alone with no one around.

One day as we were playing on the swing set, my sister noticed a black car with two people inside pointing over to us, now the car was in an alleyway behind the old woman's house, we didn't think anything about it until I saw the old woman running over to us. She looked very frightened, she then grabbed us and ran back across the street to my mother.

That's when I saw her and my mother discussing about what had happened. Now I did not have a clue as to what was going on, that's when my mother told us that we have to watch out for strangers. To me this was very strange because we never had any problems in the area, especially on my street where everyone pretty much knew each other and watched out for one another.

After the incident we still got to see grandma who would come over and visit us every now and then, everything seemed pretty normal – that is until the black car decided to come back.

One morning my sister and I was playing around the house, as usual we would argue on issues as we would normally do, but this time mother had asked us to stop arguing and watch some TV while she would take my baby brother a bath. That's when we decided to take advantage of the situation and go outside instead of being cooped up in the house. –

While playing around the front yard a car pulled up to the house, as it stopped a man opened the door and asked us if we would like some candy. The man sounded very friendly and convincing, then stated that he was a friend of my father's. Upon hearing this I felt a bit more reassuring believing that he actually was. As we walked up to the car the stranger then asked if we would like to take a ride, after all every kid would love a free ride.

We entered the car through the back door, suddenly as he started driving away, I noticed my sister looking out the back window then told me that my mother was chasing after the car. As I turned, I saw her chasing the car yelling and screaming, we shouted for him to stop but he kept going. My sister and I both looked at each other frightened and confused, at this point we didn't know what to think so we just sat there motionless, then fear and uncertainty entered our minds.

We kept yelling out to him to stop, but all he kept telling us was that everything would be okay and that he would soon go back to pick up my mother. The stranger never stopped and kept driving away, as he did so he kept reassuring us that he would take us home very soon. He continued driving until he had driven into a field where he later stopped and turned towards us, that is when he reached over and once again and offered us some candy. –

Suddenly he started unwrapping the candy and physically helped put it into our mouths, with confusion and fear I did not know what to do, nor did my sister. After taking the candy I felt very faint and dizzy, suddenly I blacked out. – –

After waking up I was still very dizzy, however I noticed that I was not at home but instead in another house with a strange woman standing over me. As I looked around I saw my sister sitting up on a sofa nearby, she also had the same experience as I did after eating the candy. – –

As I staggered to get up, I heard the woman telling us that everything would be all right. Not knowing what to think and still a bit dizzy I sat down. I looked over to my sister and asked her where are we, she was just as clueless as I was, and told me that she did not recognize the place nor the woman either.

With dizziness and confusion on our minds, we just sat there motionless, waiting until we can make some sense of what was going on. –

After a while the dizziness had worn off, I quickly got up and told my sister that we would have to get out of this strange house as soon as possible. I grabbed her hand and started towards the door, suddenly the woman yelled out and told us to stop and get back over to the sofa.

Her tone of voice had changed, she now sounded very angry and stated that, there is no place that we can run to, and that no one would help us to get back. –

Upon hearing this we were now shocked and confused more than ever, but also very frightened as to what the woman might do next. She then walked over to the TV and turned on some cartoons for us to watch, and with an angry voice she told us that dinner will be ready soon and not to give her any trouble. As we sat there watching the cartoons, we looked at each in confusion and fear, not knowing what to think or do. –

As dinner time approached the woman came back and asked us if we were hungry, as for one I can say that I was starving, after all it had been a whole day that we hadn't eaten. As we went over to the table my sister asked the woman when would we see our mother again, suddenly the woman stood up and yelled out very angrily: I'm your mother now and we are to obey her to whatever she says to do, and after dinner we better get ready for bed.

We sat there speechless throughout the dinner, not knowing what to or say we finished our dinner without saying a word and headed for bed. – –

We walked over to the bedroom where there were two beds, as we got into bed the woman told us that if we would need anything we were to ask her for it, then left the room. My sister with tears in her eyes asked me what should we do, I didn't have any answers but to tell her not to worry, and that we will leave soon, we looked at each other too afraid to cry out or say anything then drifted off to sleep.

The next morning the woman told us to dress up quickly, and mentioned that there were many things to be done in the backyard and for us to be ready as soon as possible. As we headed to the backyard, I saw piles of wood and boxes all over the place, it looked more like a junkyard. She then told us to clean up and organize the yard. –

As we worked around the yard my sister came over and showed me a large oven, it was a very old metal oven with a great big door in front of it. It reminded me of the story – Hensel and Gretel – with the old witch. I quickly turned to my sister and started teasing her that, the woman might have an idea such as in the story. My sister who was already nervous started to cry, the woman then noticed this yelled out if I continued, she would lock me up in a closet – not knowing if it were a joke or not I quickly stopped.

We pretty much stayed out doing yard work the whole day, separating and organizing the junk that littered the entire yard. As the day went on, we were pretty much exhausted and very hungry, I asked the woman if we could have something to eat, she stated that as soon as were done she would fix something for us.

It was now pretty late and dark, the woman then called us over to a fire that she had put together, it was more like a camp fire where we all sat around. She put together some sandwiches for us, then surprise us with some s'mores which tasted great. Even though she was a strange woman and we had no idea where we were or what was going on, strangely we began to accept the situation that we were in. The night went on with some lemonade and stories told by the woman.

But the comfort of the fire and storytelling was not to last.

As the night went on my sister began to feel much better, she even started joking around and stated that, she would ask the woman to put me in the oven if I kept bothering her. I then told her that I would escape from this place soon.

Upon hearing what we were saying, the woman stood up and shouted that there will be no place for us to run to. She then began shouting at us that we were ungrateful, and that we would not go anywhere. As I looked into her eyes, she looked very strange and did not resemble the same person who minutes earlier sat down with us around the fire. –

She then stated that if we tried to escape, she would tie us up and put us into the basement. After the yelling and the threats, she turned around and went into the house yelling and screaming, my sister and I froze in fear, not knowing what to do or say we just stood by each other and waited to see what would happen next.

It was sometime later when the woman came back out, and by this time it was very late and pretty cold. My sister and I sat together near the fire to keep warm, as the woman came back out, I asked her if we could go inside because of the cold, she shouted back at us stating that we should be left outside in the cold and freeze. She then stood there staring at us with a strange look on her face, my sister and I stood there motionless, at this point we were tired and cold and didn't know what else to do.

After staring at us for a while, she then told us to go back to bed. As we got back to our room, we were tired and exhausted, that is where I decided to escape through the bedroom window. I discussed the matter with my sister but she was hesitant in doing so. I told her that we must leave from here otherwise something might happen to us and we might never see our mother again.

I kept trying to convincing my sister to go out the window with me, but she was too shaken up and told me to wait for a better time, she then started crying and kept repeating to herself that she wanted to see my mother again. The woman overheard us talking then shouted out to keep quiet and go to sleep. Upon watching my sister crying, I told myself that one day, I will leave the house and take my sister with me. We later drifted off to sleep not knowing what to expect, but I knew that we couldn't stay there for long. –

The next day I woke up and saw the woman talking to a man, I don't know if he was the same one who took us into the car, however I then noticed both of them arguing, the woman then grabbed her keys walked over to us and stated that, she was going to take us to see our mother. Upon hearing this we literally jumped for joy, and was so happy and joyful to hear this. We followed her into the car and rushed into the backseat at this point nothing else mattered, we just wanted to see our mother again.

As the woman drove down the street, she asked us if we enjoyed staying over her house, now at this point we really didn't know how to answer, because we were afraid of giving the wrong answer, so we just said yes to everything.

Suddenly the woman stopped in front of a candy store and said, your mother is inside waiting for you. We rushed out the car door and ran straight into the store, as soon as we entered the store, we looked all around but my mother was nowhere to be seen. At that moment my sister broke down crying and I was halfway there myself – until the store owner came over and noticed that something was wrong.

With my sister crying and the both of us standing there alone, was more than enough for him to notice that something wasn't right. He asked us what was the problem, at this point we didn't even know what to say anymore. As he tried to calm us down, I mentioned to him about the strange woman driving us here and had told us that our mother would be in here. Upon hearing all this, he told us that he would call the police.

It was several minutes later when I saw two policemen coming over to us, they asked if we were both all right, then surprised us by stating our names, a feeling of relief and joy came over us. The police officer then told us that they have been looking for us for quite some time, and mentioned that he would be taking us back home where our parents were waiting for us. As you could imagine, we jumped up and down with relief, then ran into the police car knowing that we were finally going back home. –

On our way home the police officers kept asking us, if we knew who it was that kidnapped us, and if we knew which house where we were kept. As usual we had no clue as to who the woman was or where the house was located, all we knew is that we were so glad to get away from there. – –

It was several minutes later when we approached our house, I could see police cars all around the area along with a helicopter flying overhead. That was probably the most exciting part for me, however there were also news reporters with cameras all over the place, not to mention all of the neighbors that came out to greet us. As we approached the house, we could see my parents who were right in front waiting for us. Upon seeing this my sister broke down crying, especially as the police car got closer to my mother.

But the best part was when I saw my mother, standing alongside my father as we drove up to the house, they were surrounded by family members, all of which were crying and glad to see that we were home at last. My mother came running over to us and fell down to her knees, then grabbed us so hard that she didn't want to let go. I couldn't forget the expression on her face, and I cannot describe the feeling that I had when I saw her.

It was a very emotional time for everyone, I remembered the news reporters trying to interview us, but with all that was going on, we were all so tired and exhausted of the whole thing, especially for me and my sister. At this point all we wanted to do was get back to our lives, and the feeling of being back home was wonderful, I cannot describe to you the feeling of being back home again, especially after what we went through.

It wasn't until much later that I found out, we were missing for four days, and that our photos were being posted on national news for being kidnapped. My father who was not in town at the time but in Cleveland Ohio, and was unaware of the whole matter until he got word from his friend, who was watching the news story on television. –

The police later tried questioning us, even took us over to a café where my father had many friends and people he knew. The police wanted to know if it was someone from that side, then the police sat us near the entrance of the café, where every time someone entered, my father and the police would ask us if we recognized them.

We never did find out who kidnapped us or as to why, but as time went on – my sister like myself forgot about the whole ordeal and moved on with our lives.

It was a couple of years later when my parents decided to move to New York City, I had no clue of what New York City was. I thought it was a different country altogether. As the day came for us to move, my mother started packing our belongings together, she didn't take much just a few clothing and a few other items.

Everything else that meant so much to me, such as my bicycle and other personal belongings was left behind. I asked about why were we moving and why couldn't I take my other belongings, but there was no answer.

As she continued packing, I grabbed one of my favorite police cars that I had, the flashing lights with the siren would be displayed when turned on, however being in a hurry I then grabbed the car and placed it into the luggage accidentally turning it on. This would stay on for quite some time and later would have a little surprise when we landed.

At the same time we were packing up, my sister came in and mentioned that my friends were outside waiting to say goodbye. As I went out to meet them, I saw that they were standing there with a blank look on their faces, a feeling of sadness went through me, so to the expression on my friends faces.

After all, these were the friends who I had gone through so much with, and had many great times together. As I said goodbye everything felt very quiet, and we really didn't say much.

As we drove away a strange feeling came over me, it was as if a part of your life was left behind, how do I explain that – I can't.

Later as we got to the airport, my parents had some friends of theirs over to say goodbye, as they were moving the luggage around, I could hear the siren of the police car still running. Afterwards as we took flight, I remembered looking out the window of the plane and saw the farmlands of America. It was a great site for me, especially when I never seen anything like this before. Later as we approached New York City, all I could see was all those lights and great tall buildings that I have never seen before, it was very different from my home town in Dearborn, and I was very excited to see this new – country.

As we landed, we then drove over to our new home in Brooklyn, I saw for the first time a great big apartment building in which our apartment would be on the first floor on the bottom. I ran over to my new place, and it was totally different from what I had before. As my parents started unloading the luggage, suddenly to my surprise I saw the police car with its lights and siren still on. But by now because it was on the entire time the batteries had died out, however it stayed on just enough until I got into my new home. – Coincidence right?

As time went on, I went over to a new school where I met new friends, and like everything else in life you move on, nothing stays the same. But the times that I had growing up in Michigan would never leave my mind, and it is those times that would never change. –

It was years later when I decided to visit my old neighborhood in Dearborn, and found that the places and people of your past may change, but the fond memories that you had experienced will always be there with you.

I hope you enjoyed my adventures, for each of the stories are true accounts of what I had experienced as a kid in Michigan. And it was just as fun writing this book and to have shared those moments with you.

THE END

Printed in the United States
by Baker & Taylor Publisher Services